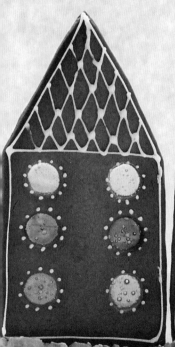

holiday
cupcakes &
cookies

holiday
cupcakes &
cookies

RYLAND PETERS & SMALL
LONDON • NEW YORK

Senior Designer Iona Hoyle
Editor Ellen Parnavelas
Production Meskerem Berhane
Art Director Leslie Harrington
Editorial Director Julia Charles

Indexer Vanessa Bird

First published in 2013 by Ryland Peters & Small
20–21 Jockey's Fields
London WC1R 4BW
and
519 Broadway, 5th Floor
New York, NY 10012

www.rylandpeters.com

10 9 8 7 6 5 4 3 2 1

Text © Hannah Miles, Chloe Coker and
Annie Rigg 2013
Design and photographs
© Ryland Peters & Small 2013

Printed in China

UK ISBN: 978-1-84975-430-9
US ISBN: 978-1-84975-456-9

CIP records for this book are available from the
British Library and the US Library of Congress.

notes

• All spoon measurements are level unless
otherwise specified.

• Eggs used in this book are UK medium/
US large, unless otherwise specified.

• Ovens should be preheated to the specified
temperatures. All ovens work slightly differently.
We recommend using an oven thermometer and
suggest you consult the maker's handbook for
any special instructions, particularly if you are
cooking in a fan-assisted/ convection oven, as
you will need to adjust temperatures according
to manufacturer's instructions.

• All cupcakes will store for up to 2 days in an
airtight container, unless otherwise stated in
the recipe.

Photography credits

All photography by William Lingwood, except
pages 44, 47, 58, 59, 61 (Laura Edwards), pages
8, 50–54, 56, 57, jacket spine and endpapers
(Tara Fisher), pages 2, 10 insert, 12–13 inserts,
42, 45, 46, 49, jacket front above right and
below left (Martin Norris), page 62 (Steve
Painter), pages 9, 11 insert, 48, 55, 60, 63
(Kate Whitaker) and jacket front centre insert
Jo Tyler.

Special thanks to:

Prop Stylist Liz Hippisley

Food Stylists Bridget Sargeson &

Jack Sargeson

food colouring & flavouring suppliers

UK

Jane Asher, for food colourings and
sugarcraft supplies
www.jane-asher.co.uk

Squires, for food colourings (pastes and
powders) and various flavouring extracts
www.squires-shop.com

US

Global Sugar Art, for cake decorating supplies
www.globalsugarart.com

contents

introduction • 6

cupcakes • 14

cookies • 42

gingerbread & brownies • 50

index • 64

introduction

Cupcakes and cookies are made for sharing and what could be more festive than baking some delicious treats to fill your home with the warming, spiced smells of Christmas? At this time of year, everything takes on a magical sparkle and feels that little bit more special, and baking is no exception. Giving and receiving are such an important part of the holidays and home-baked gifts packaged in boxes and wrapped in pretty paper and ribbons are guaranteed to bring joy to all those lucky enough to receive them. There is something here for everyone, so whether you are a novice baker or an expert, there is no end to the delights that you can whip up at this creative time of year. This book will help you make the most of the holiday season, so put on some festive music, decorate the tree and get together with family and friends to bake some delicious treats to enjoy together.

vanilla cookie dough

This dough makes lovely crumbly, buttery cookies. It is delicious as it is, but if chocolate is your favourite, you can replace 60 g/½ cup of the flour with cocoa powder to make rich, dark chocolate cookies instead.

250 g/2½ cups plain/all-purpose flour

125 g/1¼ cups self-raising/rising flour

pinch of salt

250 g/2 sticks unsalted butter, at room temperature

125 g/⅔ cup unrefined superfine sugar

1 egg yolk

1 teaspoon vanilla extract

Sift the flours and salt into a mixing bowl and set aside.

Cream the butter and sugar in another bowl until light and fluffy. Beat in the egg yolk and vanilla extract until they are fully incorporated. Add the flours and mix everything together until all the flour is incorporated and the mixture forms a dough. Stop mixing as soon as the flour is incorporated, as you do not want to overwork the dough.

Put the dough in a sealable food bag and chill in the fridge for at least 1 hour.

Roll out the cookie dough on a clean, lightly-floured work surface using a rolling pin. Stamp out as many cookies as you can from the dough with a cookie cutter of your choice. Put the cookies on a lined baking sheet and chill in the fridge for 30 minutes.

Meanwhile, preheat the oven to 200°C (400°F) Gas 6.

Bake for 12–16 minutes until the cookies are golden and smell baked.

gingerbread cookie dough

Gingerbread is a great cookie dough, because it makes the house smell wonderful and keeps really well, both baked and unbaked. It is also an easy recipe to personalize. This recipe makes a gently spiced cookie with a hint of citrus, but you can change the quantities of spices to suit your tastes and even add a pinch of ground pepper for some extra zing.

125 g/1 stick unsalted butter

100g/½ cup dark soft brown sugar

2 tablespoons water

2 tablespoons golden syrup/ light corn syrup

1 tablespoon treacle/molasses

250 g/2½ cups plain/ all-purpose flour

½ teaspoon bicarbonate of soda/baking soda

100 g /1 cup self-raising/ self-rising flour

1 tablespoon ground ginger

2 teaspoons ground cinnamon

2 teaspoons mixed spice/ apple pie spice

finely grated zest of 1 orange or lemon (optional)

Put the butter, sugar, water, syrup and molasses in a heavy-based saucepan and melt over a low heat, stirring occasionally. Remove from the heat and leave to cool for a few minutes.

Meanwhile, sift the flours, baking soda, and all the spices together into a large bowl and add the citrus zest, if using.

Make a well in the middle of the dry ingredients and pour in the melted mixture. Gently stir in the flour, so that there are no lumps, until the mixture comes together to form a soft dough.

Roll out the cookie dough on a clean, lightly-floured work surface using a rolling pin. Stamp out as many cookies as you can from the dough with a cookie cutter of your choice. Put the cookies on a lined baking sheet and chill in the fridge for 30 minutes.

Meanwhile, preheat the oven to 200°C (400°F) Gas 6.

Bake for 8–12 minutes until the cookies are golden and smell baked.

icing techniques

Royal icing is traditionally made with egg whites, but if you want to avoid using raw eggs, there are two options open to you (see below). Always make sure your mixing bowl is clean and free of grease. There are two main ways to cover a cookie: flooding it with royal icing or covering it with rolled fondant icing (sugarpaste). Both methods produce lovely results and are often interchangeable, depending on your personal preference.

royal icing

2 extra large egg whites

450 g /3¼ cups icing/ confectioners' sugar

2 teaspoons lemon juice

Put the egg white and lemon juice in a large, clean, mixing bowl. Slowly add the icing/confectioners' sugar, mixing it gently by hand or on a slow speed in food processor until incorporated. Increase the speed to medium and beat the icing for 5–10 minutes until it turns bright white and glossy and holds its shape like a stiff meringue.

outlining cookies

When piping icing, make sure the top of the piping bag is tightly folded down so that the bag is taut. The pressure should be coming from the top of the bag, so squeeze the bag from the top, not the middle, using your dominant hand. You may want to use the fingers of your other hand to steady the bag. The purpose of the outline is to create a barrier to hold the flooding icing on the cookie. With your first few projects, you may want to use a wider nozzle (Wilton size 4) to make a thicker barrier so that the icing is less likely to overflow. As you get more confident, you will be able use a narrow nozzle (Wilton size 1–2), which gives a more subtle outline.

When outlining the cookie, pipe as close to the edge of the cookie as possible. Hold the bag at a 45-degree angle, apply even pressure, and move the bag steadily along the cookie.

For best results, lift the tip off the cookie and allow the icing to fall, rather than dragging the tip along the surface of the cookie.

Don't worry if it goes wrong: the icing will be fairly elastic and you will be able to move it with a cocktail stick/toothpick or use a damp paintbrush to tidy your icing. Although the neater the better, don't worry if your outline is not perfect, provided there are no gaps in it. Once the cookie is flooded, you won't notice any minor imperfections. Leave the outline to dry for a few minutes before flooding the cookie (see opposite).

flooding with icing

With this method, the icing dries very hard to give the cookie a smooth, professional finish. It is a more complicated and time-consuming method than using rolled fondant, but it produces beautiful results. This is the method used by many professional cookie makers.

Flooded cookies are made in two stages: first they are outlined with piping icing and then they are flooded with flooding icing. Both types of icing are made from the same basic royal icing recipe (see opposite). As a guide, you will need one-third of the icing in each flooded recipe to outline the cookies and the other two-thirds to flood them.

Use the icing as it is to outline the cookies, but for flooding you will need to thin it with a little water until it reaches the consistency of emulsion paint. Add water a teaspoonful at a time until you get the right consistency

Spread some icing onto the cookie, keeping it away from the edges. Spread enough icing onto the cookie so that it looks generously covered, but not so much that it overflows.

Use a round-bladed knife to guide the icing so that it floods any gaps.

Once you have flooded the cookie, check the surface for any air bubbles and pop them with a cocktail stick/toothpick. Note that if you start flooding your cookies and realize that the consistency is not quite right, it is better to stop and fix it rather than persevering, as the results will never be satisfactory.

special effects

Rolled fondant, also available as ready-to-roll icing, is perfect for decorating cakes and cookies. It is sold in most good cake shops and supermarkets.

covering with rolled fondant

Using rolled fondant provides a very quick and easy way to decorate cakes and cookies and is ideal for children, as it is not as complicated as flooding with royal icing. If the icing does not stick, and you have no edible glue, use a little corn syrup or sugar syrup made from dissolving sugar and warm water on a 1:1 ratio and brushing over the cookies.

Work the icing between your fingers until it is pliable. Try not to use your palms, as they will make the icing sticky. To colour the icing, put some food colouring on a cocktail stick/toothpick and put it in the icing, then knead the icing until the colour is fully blended with no streaks.

Roll the icing out on a clean work surface dusted with icing/confectioners' sugar to a 3 mm/⅛ inch thickness. Then cut the icing into your chosen shapes using a cookie cutter, or a sharp knife. If the icing is not too dry, it will stick to the cookie or cake; alternatively, brush the cookie with edible glue using a damp brush.

Attach the icing to the cookie or cake. If the cookie has spread a little in the oven, lightly roll over the icing to stretch it right to the edges of the cookie or cake. Finally, run your finger around the edge of the icing to smooth it on for a perfect finish.

polka dots

Polka-dot and striped rolled fondant look great on cookies. To make polka-dot icing, roll out some white icing as normal. Then roll some small balls of coloured icing between your fingers and squash these down onto the white icing using your thumb. When all the balls are in place, gently roll over the icing with a rolling pin to incorporate the dots into the white icing.

bows

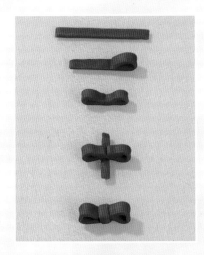

Once you have learnt to make the icing bows, you can use them on all sorts of different cakes and cookies. If you don't have time to make fondant bows, real ribbons tied around cakes and cookies makes a beautiful decoration as well.

Dust a clean work surface with icing/confectioners' sugar. Make some polka-dot rolled fondant using the technique on page 12. Cut out squares of rolled fondant the same size as the cookies.

To make a bow, cut out a strip of red rolled fondant about 1 cm/⅜ inch wide and twice the length that you would like the bow to be. Take one end and fold it into the middle, making sure that the curl stands open (you can use the end of a paintbrush or some rolled-up paper towels to support it). Fold in the other half so that the ends meet in the middle.

Lay the bow on another, slightly thinner, strip of rolled fondant. Fold in the ends of this strip and turn the bow over. Finally, gently squeeze the sides to shape the bow.

To make the ribbon tails, cut a strip of rolled fondant 1 cm/⅜ inch wide. Cut it in half and cut little triangles in the ends. Attach the strips to the centre of the cookie and stick the bow on top.

stripes

To make stripes, roll out some coloured icing and some white icing to a 3 mm/⅛ inch thickness. Cut the white icing into thin strips and lay them over the coloured icing. Roll over the strips to incorporate.

Cupcakes

These little cupcakes, flavoured with Christmas spices and topped with golden marzipan and sugar holly leaves look like mini Christmas cakes. They are perfect for a celebratory afternoon tea.

holly berry

Basic Cake Mixture

- 125 g/1 stick butter, softened
- 115 g/½ cup caster sugar
- 2 eggs
- 115 g/1 cup self raising/rising flour, sifted
- 2 tablespoons buttermilk
- 1 teaspoon vanilla extract

Flavourings

- 1 teaspoon ground mixed spice
- 1 teaspoon ground cinnamon
- 2 heaped tablespoons sultanas/golden raisins

For the topping

- 400 g/14 oz. white, ready-to-roll icing
- green food colouring
- icing/confectioners' sugar for dusting
- 240 g/9 oz. golden marzipan
- 4 tablespoons apricot jam
- 72 small red sugar balls

Equipment

- 12-hole cupcake pan filled with cupcake cases
- small holly cutter
- 7-cm/3-inch round cookie cutter

Makes 12

Preheat the oven to 180°C (350°F) Gas 4.

Put the butter and sugar in a mixing bowl and beat together using a whisk or hand-held mixer until light and creamy. Add the eggs and beat again. Fold in the flour, buttermilk and vanilla using a spatula or a large spoon.

Fold the spices and sultanas/golden raisins into the cake mixture using a spatula or large spoon. Spoon the mixture into the cupcake cases and bake for 15–20 minutes until the cakes spring back to your touch. Remove from the oven and let cool on a wire rack.

Colour 160 g/5½ oz. of the ready-to-roll icing with a little green food colouring, then roll out on a clean work surface dusted with icing/confectioners' sugar using a rolling pin. Cut out 144 holly leaves using the holly cutter.

Roll out the remaining white ready-to-roll icing and cut out 12 circles, using the round cutter. Roll out the marzipan and cut out 12 circles, using the same cutter. Heat the apricot jam in a saucepan and brush the top of each cooled cake with the jam using a pastry brush. Put a marzipan circle on top of each cake and press down firmly with your fingertips. Brush the top of the marzipan with a little more apricot jam and top with an icing circle, again pressing down to secure in place. Fix 12 holly leaves in pairs on top of each cake using a little of the apricot jam. Put 2 or 3 red sugar balls at the top of each pair of holly leaves and fix in place with your fingertips.

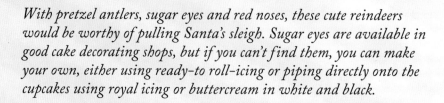

With pretzel antlers, sugar eyes and red noses, these cute reindeers would be worthy of pulling Santa's sleigh. Sugar eyes are available in good cake decorating shops, but if you can't find them, you can make your own, either using ready-to roll-icing or piping directly onto the cupcakes using royal icing or buttercream in white and black.

red-nose reindeer

1 quantity Basic
Cake Mixture
(see page 15)

For the topping
250 g/9 oz. dark/
bittersweet chocolate,
melted
12 red sugar dragees or candies
24 sugar eyes
24 salted pretzels

Equipment
12-hole cupcake pan filled with
cupcake cases
Makes 12

Preheat the oven to 180°C (350°F) Gas 4.

Spoon the cake mixture into the cupcake cases and bake for 15–20 minutes until the cakes spring back to your touch. Remove from the oven and let cool on a wire rack.

Spread the melted chocolate over the top of each cake using a round bladed knife. Before the chocolate has set, put a red candy in the middle of each cake for the reindeer's nose and fix 2 sugar eyes above the nose. Cut away one of the curves of each pretzel to make them look like antlers and put 2 at the top of each cake. Leave to set before serving.

Making snowmen in the garden is one of nicest things to do when it snows, for adults and children alike. These cupcakes are decorated with cute meringue snowmen in homage to their icy counterparts. Although the snowmen take a while to cook, they can be prepared up to a week in advance and can just be decorated at the last minute.

snowmen

1 quantity Basic Cake Mixture (see page 15)

For the snowmen

1 egg white

60 g/¼ cup caster/superfine sugar

For the topping

250 g/2 cups icing/confectioners' sugar

6 tablespoons long, shredded, soft coconut

150 g/5½ oz. ready-to-roll icing, coloured blue

black edible pen

orange decorating gel

Equipment

12-hole cupcake pan filled with cupcake cases

Makes 12

Preheat the oven to 140°C (275°F) Gas 1.

To make the snowmen, put the egg white in clean mixing bowl and whisk to stiff peaks using an electric whisk. Add the sugar a little at a time, whisking constantly until glossy and peaked. Spoon the meringue into the piping bag fitted with the large, round nozzle and pipe 12 mounds of meringue about 3 cm/1½ inches in diameter. Pipe a smaller round ball on top of each meringue mound to make a snowman shape. Bake in the oven for about 45–60 minutes until the meringues are crisp. Check towards the end of cooking as they can start to crack. Remove from the oven and set aside to cool. These can be stored in an airtight container for up to 1 week.

Preheat the oven to 180°C (350°F) Gas 4. Spoon the cake mixture into the cupcake cases and bake for 15–20 minutes until the cakes spring back to your touch. Remove from the oven and cool the cakes on a wire rack.

Mix all but 3 tablespoons of the icing/confectioners' sugar with a few drops of blue food colouring and 2–3 tablespoons of water to make a stiff icing. Using a round bladed knife, spread the icing over the top of each cupcake. Sprinkle the cakes with the coconut to look like snow. Roll out the blue ready-to-roll icing on a clean work surface dusted with icing/confectioners' sugar. Cut it into thin strips and fix 1 longer strip around each snowman's neck to make a scarf. Fix 2 shorter strips at the front, just below each snowman's head and score thin lines at the end of each using a sharp knife. Draw on black dots for eyes, buttons and mouth using the edible pen and use the decorating gel to create a carrot shape for each snowman's nose. Fix the snowmen on top of the cakes using a little of the icing and dust with edible glitter to serve.

These little cakes are decorated to look like snowy tree-lined mountain tops and are as pretty as a postcard. If you want to be more adventurous, you can add sugar house shapes to the tops of the cakes as well as the trees.

snow scene

1 quantity Basic Cake Mixture
(see page 15)

For the topping

80 g/3 oz. ready-to-roll icing,
coloured green

500 g/4 cups royal
icing/confectioners'
sugar, sifted, plus extra
for dusting

1 teaspoon vanilla extract

silver or white sugar balls

edible glitter (optional)

Equipment

muffin pan filled with 8
muffin cases

small Christmas tree cutter

Makes 8

Begin by making the Christmas tree decorations. Using a rolling pin, roll out the green ready-to-roll icing very thinly on clean work surface dusted with icing/confectioners' sugar. Cut out approximately 40–45 Christmas trees using the cutter. Leave to dry before using, preferably overnight.

Preheat the oven to 180°C (350°F) Gas 4.

Spoon the cake mixture into the muffin cases and bake for 15–20 minutes until the cakes spring back to your touch. Remove from the oven and cool the cakes on a wire rack.

Whisk the royal icing/confectioners' sugar with 85 ml/⅓ cup water and the vanilla until the icing is voluminous and stands in stiff peaks. Add a little more water if the icing is too thick. Using a round bladed knife, spread the icing on top of the cakes and swirl into peaks so it looks like a snow scene. Add the sugar trees and silver balls and sprinkle with edible glitter, if using. Allow the icing to set before serving.

Tiny sugar gingerbread men are such a simple yet cute decoration for these festive spiced cupcakes. If you do not have sugar gingerbread decorations, you can buy or make small gingerbread cookies and place one of top of each cake instead.

gingerbread men

1 quantity Basic Cake Mixture (see page 15)
1 teaspoon ground cinnamon
1 teaspoon ground ginger
1 tablespoon gingerbread syrup

For the topping
60 ml/¼ cup buttermilk
1 tablespoon gingerbread syrup
2 teaspoons ground cinnamon
350 g/3 cups icing/confectioners' sugar, sifted
125 g/1 stick butter, softened
sugar gingerbread men decorations
mini silver balls

Equipment
12-hole cupcake pan filled with cupcake cases
piping bag fitted with a large star nozzle
Makes 12

Preheat the oven to 180°C (350°F) Gas 4.

Fold the cinnamon, ginger and syrup into the cake mixture using a spatula or large spoon. Spoon the mixture into the cupcake cases and bake for 15–20 minutes until the cakes spring back to your touch. Remove from the oven and cool the cakes on a wire rack.

To make the topping, whisk the buttermilk, syrup, cinnamon, icing/confectioners' sugar and butter together in a mixing bowl until light, creamy and holding soft peaks. Add a little extra icing sugar if the mixture is soft. Spoon the icing into the piping bag and pipe a swirl of icing on top of each cupcake. Top the cakes with the sugar gingerbread men and silver balls. Leave to set before serving.

Peppermint bark is an American Christmas tradition and is truly delicious. Rather than making slices of peppermint bark, you can use it as a festive topping for these chocolate chip cupcakes.

peppermint bark

1 quantity Basic Cake Mixture (see page 15)

2 tablespoons cocoa powder, sifted

100 g/3½ oz. milk chocolate chips

For the topping

240 g/9 oz. white chocolate

1 teaspoon peppermint essence

4 candy canes, crushed or red and white peppermint candies

Equipment

12-hole cupcake pan filled with cupcake cases

Makes 12

Preheat the oven to 180°C (350°F) Gas 4.

Fold the cocoa and chocolate chips into the cake mixture. Spoon the mixture into the cupcake cases and bake for 15–20 minutes until the cakes spring back to your touch. Remove from the oven and cool the cakes on a wire rack.

Break the white chocolate into small pieces and put it in a heatproof bowl over a pan of barely-simmering water. Take care that no water gets into the chocolate as it can affect the melting properties of the chocolate. Allow the chocolate to melt, stirring occasionally, then mix in the peppermint essence. Finely chop the candy canes into small pieces.

Spoon the melted white chocolate over the top of each cupcake and spread out with a round bladed knife. Sprinkle with the candy cane pieces and leave to set before serving.

These cupcakes are inspired by the dance of the Sugar Plum fairy in the seasonal favourite ballet The Nutcracker. With a slow roasted plum in the middle and decorated with pretty candies, these cupcakes are a perfect Christmas treat.

sugar plum

4 fresh plums

1 quantity Basic Cake Mixture (see page 15)

1 teaspoon ground cinnamon

For the topping

350 g/3 cups icing/confectioners' sugar, sifted

60 ml/¼ cup milk

125 g/1 stick butter, softened

pink food colouring

Turkish delight, marshmallows and liquorish allsorts or other candies, to decorate

edible glitter (optional)

Equipment

ovenproof dish

muffin pan filled with 8 muffin cases

piping bag fitted with a large star nozzle

Makes 8

Preheat the oven to 140°C (275°F) Gas 1.

Cut the plums in half, remove the stones/pits and put the plum halves cut-side down in an ovenproof dish. Add a few spoons of water to the dish and slow roast the plums for about 2 hours until soft. Leave to cool.

Preheat the oven to 180°C (350°F) Gas 4.

Fold the cinnamon into the cake mixture. Put a spoonful of cake mixture into each of the cupcake cases. Add a roasted plum half to each filled cake case, pressing the plum down gently. Cover completely with another spoonful of cake mixture then bake for 15–20 minutes until the cakes spring back to your touch. Remove from the oven and cool the cakes on a wire rack.

To make the topping, whisk together the icing/confectioners' sugar, milk and butter until very light and creamy. Whisk in a few drops of food colouring until you have a pale pink icing. Spoon the icing into the piping bag and pipe a large swirl of icing on top of each of the cakes. Decorate with the candies and sprinkle with edible glitter, if using.

These pretty little parcel cakes have a shiny glazed icing and are piped with bows. They are tiny morsels of sweet cake, with a hazelnut buttercream guaranteed to delight any guest. If you cannot find hazelnut butter, substitute peanut butter instead.

Christmas fancies

1 quantity Basic Cake Mixture (see page 15)

For the buttercream

300 g/2½ cups icing/confectioners' sugar

60 g/4 tablespoons butter, softened

1–2 tablespoons milk

1 tablespoon hazelnut butter

For the topping

800 g/6½ cups fondant icing/confectioners' sugar

food colouring in colours of your choice

Equipment

20-cm/8-inch square cake pan, greased and lined

piping bag fitted with small, round nozzle

silver cake cases

Makes 16

Preheat the oven to 180°C (350°F) Gas 4.

Spoon the cake mixture into the prepared cake pan and bake for 20–25 minutes until the cake is golden brown and springs back to your touch. Remove from the oven and allow to cool.

To make the buttercream, whisk the icing/confectioners' sugar, butter, milk and hazelnut butter together in a mixing bowl until light and creamy. Cut the cake in half horizontally using a sharp knife. Put the bottom half of the cake on a board or tray small enough to fit in the fridge. Spread over a layer of buttercream. Put the top half of the cake on top of the buttercream layer and cover the whole cake with a thin layer of buttercream. Chill in the fridge for 2 hours until the buttercream is set firm then cut the cake into the 16 equal squares.

To make the topping, heat the fondant icing/confectioners' sugar in a saucepan until just warm, adding 125 ml/½ cup water a little at a time. You need a thick icing so you may not need to add all of the water. Reserve a little of the icing to make the bows. Stir in food colouring(s) of your choice.

Spoon the warm, white icing over the cakes, making sure that each cake is covered completely. It is best to place the cakes on a cooling rack for this with foil underneath to catch the icing drips. Leave the icing to set. Spoon the reserved, coloured icing into the piping bag and pipe a cross of icing over the top of each iced cake. Pipe a bow in the centre of each cross. Leave to set then cut the cakes from the rack by sliding a sharp knife underneath them. Put the cakes in pretty silver cake cases to serve.

Advent wreaths are traditionally lit on the four Sundays before Christmas. Topped with small white candles and red sugar flours, these cupcakes look so pretty when lit and are perfect for a gathering with family and friends.

advent wreaths

1 quantity Basic Cake Mixture (see page 15)

zest of 1 lemon

For the icing

225 g/scant 2 cups fondant icing/confectioners' sugar

1–2 tablespoons lemon juice

For the topping

225 g/scant 2 cups icing/confectioners' sugar

1 heaped tablespoon butter, softened

green food colouring

1–2 tablespoons milk

48 red sugar flowers

small gold sugar balls

Equipment

12-hole cupcake pan filled with cupcake cases

piping bag fitted with a small star nozzle

48 small candles

Makes 12

Preheat the oven to 180°C (350°F) Gas 4.

Fold the lemon zest into the cake mixture using a spatula or large spoon. Spoon the mixture into the cupcake cases and bake for 15–20 minutes until the cakes spring back to your touch. Remove from the oven and cool the cakes on a wire rack.

Mix the fondant icing/confectioners' sugar with the lemon juice to make a thick icing, adding the juice gradually as you may not need it all. Spread over the top of each cake and leave to set.

To make the topping, whisk together the icing/confectioners' sugar, butter and milk with a few drops of green food colouring until light and creamy. Add the milk gradually as you may not need it all. Spoon the buttercream into the piping bag and pipe a ring of small, green rosettes on top of each cake. Top each buttercream rosette with a golden ball and top each cake with 4 red sugar flowers. Insert 4 candles into each wreath and light the candles as you serve the cakes.

Shredded coconut makes a great fluffy beard for Santa in this recipe. If you are not able to find shredded coconut, you can also use buttercream piped in balls to make santa's beard instead.

smiling santa cupcakes

1 quantity Basic Cake Mixture
(see page 15)

For the topping

480 g/1 lb. 1 oz. white ready-to-roll icing

2 tablespoons apricot jam

2 tablespoons icing/confectioners' sugar

red and black food colouring

6 tablespoons long, shredded, soft coconut

edible silver balls

For the buttercream

225 g/scant 2 cups icing/confectioners' sugar

1 heaped tablespoon butter, softened

1–2 tablespoons milk

Equipment

12-hole cupcake pan filled with cupcake cases

7-cm/3-inch round cutter

piping bag fitted with a small round nozzle

piping bag fitted with a star nozzle

Makes 12

Preheat the oven to 180°C (350°F) Gas 4.

Spoon the cake mixture into the cupcake cases and bake for 15–20 minutes until the cakes spring back to your touch. Remove from the oven and cool the cakes on a wire rack.

Colour 240 g/9 oz. of the ready-to-roll icing with a little red food colouring. Roll out the remaining white ready to roll icing and cut out 12 circles, using the cutter. Heat the apricot jam in a saucepan and brush over the top of each cake, using a pastry brush. Put an icing circle on top of each cake. Roll out the red icing and divide it in half. Cut out 12 crescent shapes, using a sharp knife, to be the top of the hats. Put one on top of each cake aligning with the top of the cake. Use a little apricot jam to fix the icing if it does not stick. Cut 12 curved triangles out of the remaining red icing and put one on top of each red crescent to make the fold over of Santa's hat.

To make the buttercream, whisk together the icing/confectioners' sugar, butter and milk until light and creamy. Add the milk gradually as you may not need it all. Spoon the buttercream into the piping bag with the star-shaped nozzle and pipe a line of overlapping rosettes in a rope effect to create the trim of santa's hat. Pipe a rosette on the tip of each hat to create a bobble.

Mix the icing/confectioners' sugar to a stiff paste with a few teaspoons of water and colour with the black food colouring. Spoon into the piping bag with the small, round nozzle and pipe eyes on each cake just below the hats. Add a silver ball just below the eyes to create a nose. Brush the bottom of the cakes with a little buttercream and put some shredded coconut on top to make the beard. Pipe a smile with black icing onto each cake just above the beard.

These quirky Christmas trees are made using ice cream cones, decorated with white chocolate and green coconut. They may look intricate but are actually very easy to prepare. The best thing is that you can hide some surprise candies inside the cone as an extra special treat.

Christmas tree cakes

1 quantity Basic Cake Mixture
(see page 15)

2 tablespoons cocoa
powder, sifted

To decorate

80 g/3 oz. ready-to-roll icing

icing/confectioners' sugar,
for dusting

gold dusting powder

300 g/10½ oz. dark/bittersweet
chocolate, melted

400 g/14 oz. white
chocolate, melted

green food colouring gel

230 g/3 cups long, shredded,
soft coconut

16 ice cream cones

assorted candies (optional)

edible silver balls

coloured edible sugarpaste stars

Equipment

*20-cm/4-inch square cake pan,
greased and lined*

4-cm/1½-inch round cutter

small star cutter

Makes 16

Roll out the ready-to-roll icing on a clean work surface dusted with icing/confectioners' sugar and cut out 16 small stars using the star cutter. Brush the stars with the gold dusting powder and leave them to dry, preferably overnight. The stars can be stored in an airtight container for up to a week.

Preheat the oven to 180°C (350°F) Gas 4.

Fold the cocoa into the cake mixture using a spatula or large spoon. Spoon the mixture into the prepared cake pan and bake for about 15–20 minutes until the cake springs back to your touch. Remove from the oven and set aside to cool. Once cool, cut out 16 circles of cake using the round cutter and place on a wire rack set over a sheet of foil to catch any drips. Cover each of the cakes with melted dark/bittersweet chocolate. You need to prepare the cones straight away so that they will stick to the melted chocolate.

Put the melted white chocolate in a shallow dish and stir in a little green food colouring. It is important to use a gel colour and not a liquid colour as the liquid food colouring can affect the chocolate. Colour the coconut green with a little food colouring and spread out on a plate. One by one, roll each cone in the white chocolate, spooning over chocolate to cover any gaps and then immediately roll in the coconut so that all the chocolate is covered. Fill the cones with candies, if liked, then put a cone on top of one of the chocolate cakes. Repeat with the remaining cones until all the trees are assembled.

Using a little of the melted chocolate, fix a gold star on top of each cake and add the silver balls and sugarpaste stars to resemble Christmas tree lights and decorations. These are best eaten on the day they are made.

Every year figgy puddings are an essential part of any festive family feast. These cupcakes take their inspiration from this classic pudding, containing hints of orange and spices and are topped with sugar holly leaves and berries. Serve with warm brandy custard sauce or cream for an extra Christmassy treat!

figgy puddings

1 quantity Basic Cake Mixture (see page 15)

2 tablespoons cocoa powder, sifted

100 g/3½ oz. spiced chocolate (such as Green and Black's Maya gold), chopped

zest of 1 orange

1 teaspoon ground cinnamon

To decorate

200 g/7 oz. white ready-to-roll icing

green food colouring

300 g/10½ oz. dark/bittersweet chocolate, melted

8 red jelly beans

icing/confectioners' sugar, for dusting

Equipment

muffin pans lined with 8 muffin cases

large holly cutter

Makes 8

Preheat the oven to 180°C (350°F) Gas 4.

Fold the cocoa, chopped chocolate, orange zest and cinnamon into the cake mixture using a spatula or large spoon. Spoon the mixture into the muffin cases and bake for 15–20 minutes until the cakes spring back to your touch. Remove from the oven and cool the cakes on a wire rack.

Colour 50 g/1¾ oz. of the ready-to-roll icing with a little green food colouring. Roll out thinly on a clean work surface dusted with icing/confectioners' sugar and use the holly cutter to cut out 8 holly leaves. Roll out the remaining white ready to roll icing and cut out 8 circles with fluted edges to represent each pudding's icing.

Spoon the melted chocolate over the top of each cake, spreading out with a round bladed knife to make sure they are completely coated. Top each cake with the white icing and finish with 2 holly leaves. Press a red jelly bean into the middle of each cake and dust with icing/confectioners' sugar. Leave to set before serving.

The 12 days of Christmas song is the inspiration for these cute cupcakes. If you are not able to find mini marzipan pears, you can make small pear shapes with ready to roll icing and paint them yellow and red with food colouring.

partridge in a pear tree

1 quantity Basic Cake Mixture (see page 15)

For the icing

225 g/8 oz. fondant icing sugar
black food colouring

To decorate

150 g/5½ oz. ready-to-roll icing
edible gold lustre dust
marzipan sugar pears in assorted sizes
edible glitter (optional)

For the buttercream

300 g/2½ cups icing/confectioners' sugar, plus extra for dusting
2 tablespoons butter, softened
2 tablespoons milk
a few drops of green food colouring

Equipment

12-hole cupcake pan filled with cupcake cases
2 piping bags, 1 fitted with leaf nozzle and 1 fitted with small, round nozzle

Makes 12

Preheat the oven to 180°C (350°F) Gas 4.

Spoon the cake mixture into the cupcake cases and bake for 15–20 minutes until the cakes spring back to your touch. Remove from the oven and let cool on a wire rack.

Mix the fondant icing/confectioners' sugar with 1–2 tablespoons of water to make a thick icing. Spread the icing over the top of each cake, reserving 2 spoonfuls, and leave to set. Colour the reserved icing with a few drops of black food colouring.

Roll out the ready-to-roll icing out on a clean work surface dusted with icing/confectioners' sugar. Cut out 12 bird shapes and 12 wings using a sharp knife. Press one wing onto each bird and brush with the edible gold lustre dust. Spoon the black icing into the piping bag fitted with the round nozzle and pipe an eye onto each bird and an outline onto each wing.

To make the buttercream, whisk together the icing/confectioners' sugar, butter and milk with a few drops of green food colouring until light and creamy. Add the milk gradually as you may not need it all. Spoon the icing into the piping bag fitted with the leaf nozzle. Pipe leaves over to the top of each cupcake. Put an icing bird in the middle and top each cake with 2 or 3 marzipan pears. Sprinkle with a little edible glitter, if using.

Snowball fight! These cute little iced mittens holding chocolate snowballs make for fun festive cake toppers. If you are short of time you can just top the cakes with white chocolate snowballs instead.

snowballs & mittens

1 quantity Basic Cake Mixture (see page 15)

2 tablespoons cocoa powder, sifted

100 g/⅔ cup white chocolate chips

For the icing

120 g/4½ oz. ready-to-roll icing

red and blue food colouring

For the buttercream

350 g/2 cups icing/confectioners' sugar, sifted

125 g/1 stick butter, softened

60 ml/¼ cup milk

To decorate

8 white chocolate truffles

3 tablespoons icing/confectioners' sugar, plus extra for dusting

white edible mimosa balls

Equipment

muffin pan filled with 8 muffin cases

3 piping bags, 2 fitted with small round nozzles and 1 with a large, round nozzle

Makes 8

Preheat the oven to 180°C (350°F) Gas 4.

Fold the cocoa and chocolate chips into the cake mixture using a spatula or large spoon. Spoon the cake mixture into the muffin cases and bake for 15–20 minutes until the cakes spring back to your touch. Remove from the oven and cool the cakes on a wire rack.

Divide the ready-to-roll icing into two and colour half red and half blue. Roll out the red and blue icings on a clean work surface dusted with icing/confectioners' sugar, using a rolling pin. Cut out 4 red and 4 blue mitten shapes from the coloured icings, using a sharp knife. Make indents on the cuffs using a cocktail stick/toothpick.

To make the buttercream, whisk together the icing/confectioners' sugar, butter and milk until light and creamy. Add the milk gradually as you may not need it all. Spoon the icing into the piping bag fitted with the large round nozzle and pipe a swirl of buttercream on top of each cake. Put a white chocolate truffle on top of each cake and position a mitten around it so that it looks like it is holding a snowball. You need to do this while the icing is still soft so that it does not crack.

Divide the icing/confectioners' sugar in half and put it into two small bowls. Mix a little water into each to form a stiff paste. Spoon into the piping bags with the small, round nozzles and pipe decorative patterns onto the mittens in corresponding colours. Scatter the buttercream with edible mimosa balls and dust with icing/confectioners' sugar and leave to set before serving.

Cookies

These bauble cookies make lovely Christmas tree decorations. Go for turquoise, red, and white for a vintage look or opt for richer colours, such as purples or reds, for a traditional festive look. Making these cookies from gingerbread makes your house smell wonderfully festive.

baubles

12 cookies made from either of the recipes on pages 8–9, using assorted bauble-shaped cookie cutters

½ recipe each white, turquoise, and red royal icing (page 10)

edible glitter

2 m/2.2 yd white ribbon

Equipment

bauble-shaped cookie cutters

3 piping bags with fine round nozzles

round-bladed knife

spatula or table knife

Makes 12

Bake a batch of bauble-shaped cookies, cutting a small hole in the top of each before baking. Outline and flood them with royal icing in colours of your choice, following the steps on pages 10–11.

Pipe simple patterns onto the cookies in different colours to decorate, using the remaining coloured royal icing left over from outlining the cookies.

While the cookies are still wet, sprinkle with edible glitter. To get a light, even covering, put some glitter on the end of a spatula or table knife and gently tap the side of the knife while holding it over the cookies.

Finally, thread ribbon through the cookies so that they can be hung up.

These colourful parcels make a lovely Christmas gift. Once you have learnt to make the icing bows, you can use them on all sorts of different cakes and cookies. If you don't have time to make fondant bows, simply cover the cookies with rolled fondant and tie real ribbons around them.

polka-dot parcels

12 cookies made from either of the recipes on pages 8–9, using a square cookie cutter

icing/confectioners' sugar, for dusting

200 g/7 oz. white rolled fondant

200g/7 oz. red rolled fondant

edible glue

Equipment

square cookie cutter

rolling pin

knife

Makes 12

Dust a clean work surface with icing/confectioners' sugar. Make some polka-dot rolled fondant using the technique on page 12. Cut out squares of rolled fondant the same size as the cookies.

Cover the cookies with the polka-dot rolled fondant, following the steps on page 12. Roll out some more red rolled fondant to a 3 mm/⅛ inch thickness and cut strips of icing about 1 cm/⅜ inches wide. Attach 2 strips to each cookie to make the ribbons.

Make the red fondant bows using the technique on page 13.

Attach the ribbon tails to the middle of the cookies and stick the bows on top.

These flooded cookies give a vintage twist to the traditional tree, with soft colours, hearts dots, and buttons, plus trailing tinsel. They look lovely made with a gingerbread base and ivory flooded icing.

Christmas trees

12 Christmas tree cookies made from the gingerbread recipe on page 9, using a tree-shaped cookie cutter

1 recipe royal icing (page 10)

½ recipe each green, red, and teal royal icing

30 g/1 oz. each green, red, and teal rolled fondant (see page 12)

white edible glitter

Equipment

3 piping bags with fine, round nozzles

round-bladed knife

paintbrush

various small decorative cutters

Makes 12

Outline and flood the cookies, following the steps on pages 10–11. Alternatively, cover the cookies with rolled fondant following the steps on page 12.

Pipe on the tinsel, then the polka dots, hearts or flowers, using the piping bags with the fine, round nozzles. For the polka dots, keep the tip close to the surface, stop squeezing and then lift off. For a heart, pipe a 'V' squeezing harder at the start and end of the 'V'. For the flowers, pipe small rings of polka dots. To correct any errors in your icing, use a damp paintbrush.

Cut out small hearts, stars, buttons and flowers from different-coloured rolled fondant and attach to the top of each cookie. Once you have decorated the cookies, sprinkle with white edible glitter for some festive sparkle.

*These fun penguins are great to make with children during the
holidays. If penguin-shaped cutters are difficult to find, you can draw
penguin shapes on pieces of parchment paper and use these as a template
or, if you're feeling brave, cut out the shapes freehand. Rolled fondant can
easily be moulded into shape, so don't worry about being too accurate.*

jolly penguins

12 cookies made from a recipe on
pages 8–9, using penguin-
shaped cutters

icing/confectioners' sugar,
for dusting

100 g/3½ oz. orange rolled
fondant (see page 12)

edible glue

250 g/9 oz. black rolled fondant

100 g/3½ oz. white rolled fondant

100 g/3½ oz. red rolled fondant

Equipment
parchment paper template
(optional)
rolling pin
knife
cocktail stick/
toothpick
Makes 12

Dust a clean work surface with icing/confectioners' sugar and roll out the
orange rolled fondant. Cut out the feet using your parchment paper template,
if using, and a sharp knife.

Attach the orange rolled fondant to the cookies using edible glue, and mark
indents on the feet with a cocktail stick/toothpick.

Roll out some black rolled fondant and cut out the penguins' bodies using your
parchment paper template, if using, and a sharp knife. Attach them to the
cookies and gently roll over each cookie to make them fit. Roll out the white
rolled fondant and cut out oval shapes using a sharp knife for the penguins'
tummies. Attach them to the cookies. Roll out the red rolled fondant and cut
out the hats. Attach a hat to each of the cookies.

To make the eyes, roll 2 small balls of white rolled fondant between your
fingers. Squash the middle of the balls to make oval shapes and then squash
them flat. Attach them to the cookies and stick 2 tiny balls of black rolled
fondant to them for the pupils.

To make the beaks, roll a ball of orange rolled fondant between your fingers.
Pinch one end of the ball to make it into a triangle shape, then squash it flat.
Attach them to the cookies.

To finish the hats, roll a ball of white rolled fondant between your fingers and
attach one to the top of each hat to make a bobble. Roll a thin sausage of
white rolled fondant and cut it into small pieces for the trim of the hats. Attach
them to the cookies and mark lines along each piece of trim with a cocktail
stick/toothpick to give it some texture.

Gingerbread & Brownies

This is a far simpler way of making a traditional gingerbread house.
Don't forget to make a fondant snowman to complete the scene!

snowy houses

2 quantities Gingerbread Cookie
Dough (see page 9)

250 g/9 oz. clear, hard,
fruit candies

plain/all-purpose flour, for dusting

Royal Icing (see page 10)

Equipment

*pieces of card to make paper
templates*

*3 baking sheets, lined with non-
stick parchment paper*

*piping bag fitted with a small,
round nozzle*

Makes 5 gingerbread houses

Prepare the Gingerbread Cookie Dough according to the recipe on page 9, stopping after you have put the dough in the fridge to chill for at least 1 hour.

Preheat the oven to 170°C (325°F) Gas 3.

Draw 5 houses of your chosen shape and size onto pieces of card and cut them out. The largest should be no bigger than about 20–30 cm/8–12 inches.

Divide the fruit candies into separate colours and place each colour in its own freezer bag. Using a rolling pin, crush the candies into small pieces.

Lightly dust a clean work surface with flour. Divide the dough into 5 pieces in sizes to correspond to the house sizes you have chosen. Roll the dough out into neat rectangles and use the templates to cut out the house shapes. Carefully slide the shapes onto the prepared baking sheets. Using a small, sharp knife or cutters, cut out windows from each house. Bake the houses in batches on the middle shelf of the preheated oven for about 5 minutes until the gingerbread is just starting to colour at the edges.

Remove the baking sheets from the oven. Carefully and neatly fill the windows with the crushed fruit candies using a dry pastry brush to brush away any stray candy pieces. Return the baking sheets to the oven and bake for a further 5 minutes until the gingerbread is golden brown and firm and the candies have melted to fill the window shapes. Allow the houses to cool completely on the baking sheets before icing.

Fill the piping bag with the royal icing and pipe lines and dots around the windows and walls of each house. Pipe tiles or snow onto the roofs. Allow to dry completely before serving. The houses look best displayed against a window so that the light shines through the 'stained-glass' windows.

These cute Santa cookies have been made using an extra-large,
simple gingerbread-man cutter. The icing is slightly more fiddly
than most cookies, but the recipe only makes 6 cookies, so it's quite
manageable and looks beautiful!

santa claus

Gingerbread Cookie Dough
(see page 9)

plain/all-purpose flour,
for dusting

Royal Icing (see page 10)

red and black food
colouring

white sugar sprinkles

Equipment

20-cm/8-inch-tall
gingerbread-man cutter

baking sheets, lined with
non-stick parchment paper

3 piping bags fitted with small,
round nozzles

Makes 6

Prepare the Gingerbread Cookie Dough according to the recipe on page 9, stopping after you have put the dough in the fridge to chill for at least 1 hour.

Preheat the oven to 170°C (325°F) Gas 3.

Lightly dust a clean work surface with flour and roll out the dough to an even thickness. Use the cutters to stamp out as many cookies as possible from the dough. Arrange the cookies on the prepared baking sheets. Bake the gingerbread in batches on the middle shelf of the preheated oven for 10–12 minutes or until firm and lightly browned at the edges. Allow the cookies to cool completely on the baking sheets before icing.

Prepare the Royal Icing according to the recipe on page 10. Spoon three quarters of the icing into a bowl and tint it red using the food colouring. Tint a further 3 tablespoons black in a small bowl. Leave the remaining icing white. Fill a piping bag with 2 tablespoons of the red icing and pipe an outline around the bottom half of each man in the shape of a pair of trousers. (See page 10–11 for instructions on outlining and flooding). Do the same in a jacket shape around the top half. Pipe an outline for a hat. Fill another piping bag with the black icing and pipe an outline for the boots. Fill another piping bag with the white icing and pipe outlines for the fur trim on the hat, collar, belt, and sleeve and trouser cuffs. Allow to dry for at least 10 minutes.

Flood the white outlines with white icing, then scatter the white sugar sprinkles over these areas. Flood the remaining areas with their corresponding colours. Allow to dry for 20 minutes. Finally, pipe white buttons down the middle of Santa's jacket, a black buckle on his belt and 2 eyes and a big red nose. Allow to dry completely before serving.

*These pretty snowflakes are perfect for decorating the house,
for giving as gifts and for eating and enjoying. Not only do
they taste great, but they look stunning hung from silvery,
decorated branches or on the Christmas tree.*

snowflakes

Basic Spiced Gingerbread
(see page 9)

plain/all-purpose flour,
for dusting

icing/confectioners' sugar,
for dusting

250 g/8 oz. ready-
to-roll icing

2 tablespoons apricot jam, warmed

4 tablespoons Royal Icing
(see page 10)

edible silver balls

Equipment
assorted snowflake cutters
*baking sheets, lined with non-stick
parchment paper*
*a piping bag fitted with a small,
round nozzle*
tiny star-shaped embossing tools
Makes 10–12

Prepare the Gingerbread Cookie Dough according to the recipe on page 9, stopping after you have put the dough in the fridge to chill for at least 1 hour.

Preheat the oven to 170°C (325°F) Gas 3.

Lightly dust a clean work surface with flour and roll out the dough to an even thickness. Use the cutters to stamp out as many cookies as possible from the dough. Arrange the cookies on the prepared baking sheets and bake the gingerbread in batches on the middle shelf of the preheated oven for 10–12 minutes or until firm and lightly browned at the edges. Allow the cookies to cool completely on the baking sheets before icing.

Lightly dust the work surface with icing/confectioners' sugar and roll out the ready-to-roll icing to a thickness of no more than 2 mm/$\frac{1}{16}$ inch. Using the same snowflake cutters as above, stamp out shapes from the icing to match your cookies. Brush apricot jam lightly over each cookie and carefully position the icing snowflakes on top. Gently press the icing snowflakes in place.

Prepare just 4 tablespoons of the Royal Icing according to the recipe on page 10. Fill the piping bag with the royal icing and pipe delicate lines across some of the snowflakes. Use the embossing tool to press delicate patterns into the fondant icing. Stick edible silver balls to the snowflakes with a dot of royal icing. Allow the royal icing to set completely before threading the cookies with ribbon.

The decoration on these stars is minimal, but add as much sparkle as you like. Once the icing has dried completely, you could serve the cookies in a towering stack as a table centrepiece.

Christmas stars

Gingerbread Cookie Dough (see page 9)

plain/all-purpose flour, for dusting

Royal Icing (see page 10)

yellow food colouring

edible gold glitter

silver sugar stars

edible silver balls

Equipment

assorted star cutters

baking sheets, lined with non-stick baking parchment

2 piping bags with small, round nozzles

Makes 10–12

Prepare the Gingerbread Cookie Dough according to the recipe on page 9, stopping after you have put the dough in the fridge to chill for at least 1 hour.

Preheat the oven to 170°C (325°F) Gas 3.

Lightly dust a clean work surface with flour and roll the dough evenly to a thickness of 2–3 mm/⅛ inch. Use the cutters to stamp out as many cookies as possible from the dough, cutting each one as close as possible to the next one. Arrange the cookies on the prepared baking sheets and bake the gingerbread in batches on the middle shelf of the preheated oven for 10–12 minutes or until firm and browned at the edges. Allow the cookies to cool completely on the baking sheets before icing.

Prepare the Royal Icing according to the recipe on page 10. Transfer about 3 tablespoons to a small bowl and tint yellow using the food colouring. Spoon the yellow icing into a piping bag and pipe outlines around each cookie. (See page 10–11 for instructions on outlining and flooding.) Allow the icing to set for 10 minutes.

Flood the insides of the outlines with the white icing. Allow to dry for 5 minutes before scattering edible glitter and sugar stars over the cookies. Pipe small dots of icing onto the point of each star and top with edible silver balls. Allow to dry completely before serving.

Keep a lookout for red and white peppermint candies to top these minty brownies. If you can't find them, you could also use striped candy canes.

mint chocolate chip

Preheat the oven to 170°C (325°F) Gas 3.

Put the chocolate and butter in a heatproof bowl set over a pan of barely simmering water. Stir until smooth and thoroughly combined. Leave to cool slightly. In a separate bowl, whisk the sugar, eggs and peppermint extract with a balloon whisk until pale and thick. Add the melted chocolate mixture and stir until combined. Sift the flour, cocoa powder and salt into a bowl and fold in until well incorporated, then stir in the chocolate chips.

Spoon the mixture into the prepared baking pan, spread level and bake on the middle shelf of the preheated oven for about 25 minutes, or until the top has formed a light crust. Remove from the oven and leave to cool completely in the pan.

Meanwhile, to make the mint buttercream, sift the icing/confectioners' sugar into a mixing bowl, add the soft butter and beat until smooth, pale and light. Add the peppermint extract and mix until combined.

Remove the cold brownie from the pan. Spread the buttercream in an even layer over the top and refrigerate until firm.

To make the chocolate glaze, put the chocolate and syrup in a heatproof bowl set over a saucepan of barely simmering water. Do not let the bottom of the bowl touch the water. Stir occasionally until the chocolate has melted and the glaze is smooth. Remove from the heat and leave to cool and thicken slightly before using.

Spread the glaze over the top of the mint buttercream and chill in the fridge until set. Cut the brownies into 16 portions and decorate with red and white peppermint candies.

For the brownies

275 g/9½ oz. dark/bittersweet
chocolate, chopped
175 g/1½ sticks butter, diced
125 g/1 cup plain/all-purpose flour
1 teaspoon ground cinnamon
2 teaspoons ground ginger
¼ teaspoon ground nutmeg
a pinch of hot chilli/chile powder
a pinch of salt
50 g/2 oz. crystallized ginger
175 g/¾ cup plus 1 tablespoon
dark muscovado/dark
brown soft sugar
2 tablespoons golden syrup /
light corn syrup
1 tablespoon treacle/molasses
4 eggs
50 g/½ cup slivered almonds, chopped
edible gold sprinkles

For the chocolate ganache

150 g/5 oz. dark/bittersweet
chocolate, finely chopped
150 ml/⅔ cup double/heavy cream
1 tablespoon light muscovado/light
brown sugar
a pinch of salt

Equipment

a 20-cm/8-inch square baking pan,
greased and lined with
greased parchment paper

Makes 16

These warmly spiced brownies taste even better if you make them a day or two before you plan to serve them — you just have to be patient!

gingerbread

Preheat the oven to 170˚C (325˚F) Gas 3.

Put the chocolate and butter in a heatproof bowl set over a saucepan of barely simmering water. Stir until smooth and thoroughly combined. Leave to cool slightly.

Sift together the flour, all the spices and the salt.

Finely chop the crystallized ginger. Lightly whisk the sugar, syrup, treacle/molasses, eggs and vanilla extract until combined. Add the melted chocolate mixture and fold in until combined. Stir the almonds and half the chopped ginger into the bowl. Fold in the sifted dry ingredients.

Pour the mixture into the prepared baking pan, spread level and bake on the middle shelf of the preheated oven for about 25 minutes, or until the brownies are set.

Remove from the oven and leave to cool completely in the pan. When cold, remove the brownies from the pan, wrap in clingfilm/plastic wrap and leave overnight before frosting.

The next day, prepare the Chocolate Ganache. Tip the chocolate into a small, heatproof bowl. Heat the cream and sugar in a small saucepan until the sugar has dissolved and the cream is just boiling. Add the salt. Pour it over over the chopped chocolate and leave to melt. Stir until smooth, then leave to cool and thicken slightly before using.

Spread the ganache over the top of the brownies, score with the tines of a fork to make a diagonal pattern, then cut into 16 squares. Scatter the rest of the chopped ginger and a few gold sprinkles over the top.

For the whoopie pies

60 g/⅓ cup sultanas/golden raisins
60 ml/¼ cup gingerbread liqueur
125 g/1 stick unsalted butter, softened
200 g/1 cup light brown soft sugar
1 large egg
320 g/2½ cups self-raising/
self-rising flour
1 teaspoon baking powder
2 teaspoons ground cinnamon
1 teaspoon ground mixed spice
1 teaspoon ground ginger
250 ml/1 cup sour cream
½ teaspoon salt
100 ml/⅓ cup hot (not boiling) water

For the ginger cream filling

125 g/1 stick unsalted butter
50 ml/3 tablespoons sour cream
350 g/2¾ cups icing/
confectioners' sugar
50 ml/3 tablespoons
gingerbread syrup

For the topping

450 g/3⅔ cups royal icing/
confectioners' sugar
white edible mimosa balls
reindeers and/or Christmas trees

two 12-hole whoopie pie pans,
greased
a piping bag fitted with
a large star nozzle

Makes 12

These whoopie pies, inspired by the German soft iced gingerbread Lebkuchen, are a perfect winter treat. If serving as part of your Christmas celebrations, why not let your imagination run wild with the decoration and serve whoopie pies in place of a traditional cake – topped with classic royal icing and decorated with snowy scenes.

gingerbread whoopie pies

Begin by soaking the sultanas/golden raisins in the gingerbread liqueur for several hours, so that they become plump and juicy.

Preheat the oven to 180°C (350°F) Gas 4. To make the pies, cream together the butter and brown sugar in a mixing bowl for 2–3 minutes using an electric hand-held mixer, until light and creamy. Add the egg, sultanas/golden raisins and their soaking liquid and mix again. Sift the flour, baking powder, and spices into the bowl and add the salt and sour cream. Whisk again until everything is incorporated. Add the hot water and whisk into the mixture.

Put a large spoonful of mixture into each hole in the prepared pans. Leave to stand for 10 minutes then bake each pan in the preheated oven for 10–12 minutes. Remove the pies from the oven, let cool slightly then turn out onto a wire rack to cool completely.

To make the icing, whisk the royal icing/confectioners' sugar with 75 ml/⅓ cup cold water for about 5 minutes, until the icing is very stiff. Put a tablespoonful of icing on 12 of the pie halves and use a fork to form it into sharp peaks. Arrange a ring of white edible mimosa balls around the outside edge then add a reindeer or Christmas tree to each pie. Leave to set.

To make the ginger cream filling, whisk together the butter, sour cream, icing/confectioners' sugar and gingerbread syrup using an electric hand-held mixer, until light and creamy. Spoon the filling into the prepared piping bag and pipe a swirl onto the un-iced pie halves. Top with the iced pie halves and serve. These are best eaten on the day they are made.

index

A
advent wreaths 31

B
bauble cookies 43
bows, fondant 13
brownies 58–61
  gingerbread brownies 60
  mint chocolate chip brownies 59
buttercream 28, 31, 39, 40, 59

C
chocolate
  chocolate vanilla cookie dough 8
  Christmas tree cupcakes 35
  figgy pudding cupcakes 36
  ganache 60
  gingerbread brownies 60
  mint chocolate chip brownies 59
  peppermint bark cupcakes 24
  red-nose reindeer cupcakes 16
  snowballs and mittens cupcakes 40
Christmas fancies 28
Christmas star cookies 56
Christmas tree cookies 47
Christmas tree cupcakes 35
coconut
  Christmas trees cupcakes 35
  snowmen cupcakes 19
cookies 42–9

baubles 43
Christmas tree 47
flooding with icing 10
gingerbread cookie dough 9
jolly penguins 48
outlining in icing 10
polka-dot parcels 44
Santa Claus gingerbread 52
vanilla cookie dough 8
cupcakes 14–41
  advent wreaths 31
  Christmas fancies 28
  Christmas trees 35
  figgy puddings 36
  holly berry 15
  partridge in a pear tree 39
  peppermint bark 24
  red-nose reindeer 16
  smiling Santas 32
  snow scene 20
  snowballs and mittens 40
  snowmen 19
  sugar plum 27

F
figgy puddings 36
fondant icing
  bows 13
  covering cakes and cookies with 12
  polka dots 12
  stripes 13

G
ganache 60
gingerbread 50–7
  Christmas star cookies 56
  gingerbread brownies 60
  gingerbread cookie dough 9
  gingerbread men cupcakes 23

gingerbread whoopie pies 63
Santa Claus gingerbread cookies 52
snowflakes 55
snowy houses 51

H
hazelnut butter
  Christmas fancies 28
  holly berry cupcakes 15

I
icing
  bows 13
  covering with rolled fondant 12
  flooding cookies with icing 11
  outlining cookies 10
  polka dots 12
  royal icing 10
  special effects 12–13
  stripes 13
  techniques 10–13

J
jolly penguins cookies 48

M
meringues
  snowmen cupcakes 19
mint chocolate chip brownies 59

P
partridge in a pear tree cupcakes 39
penguin cookies, jolly 48

peppermint
  mint chocolate chip brownies 59
peppermint bark cupcakes 24
piping icing 10
plums
  sugar plum cupcakes 27
polka-dot parcel cookies 44
polka dots, icing 12

R
raisins: holly berry cupcakes 15
red-nose reindeer cupcakes 16
royal icing 10

S
Santa Claus gingerbread cookies 52
smiling Santa cupcakes 32
snow scene cupcakes 20
snowballs and mittens cupcakes 40
snowflake gingerbread 55
snowmen cupcakes 19
snowy house gingerbread 51
sour cream
  gingerbread whoopie pies 63
spiced cupcakes
  figgy puddings 36
  gingerbread men cupcakes 23
  holly berry cupcakes 15
star gingerbread, Christmas 56
stripes, icing 13
sugar plum cupcakes 27
sugarpaste *see* fondant icing

V
vanilla cookie dough 8